Home is Not Lost

poems by

Jean B. Fleischauer

Finishing Line Press
Georgetown, Kentucky

Home is Not Lost

Copyright © 2023 by Jean B. Fleischauer
ISBN 979-8-88838-302-5 First Edition
All rights reserved under International and Pan-American Copyright Conventions. No part of this book may be reproduced in any manner whatsoever without written permission from the publisher, except in the case of brief quotations embodied in critical articles and reviews.

Publisher: Leah Huete de Maines
Editor: Christen Kincaid
Cover Art: Jean B. Fleischauer
Author Photo: Jean B. Fleischauer
Cover Design: Elizabeth Maines McCleavy

Order online: www.finishinglinepress.com
also available on amazon.com

Author inquiries and mail orders:
Finishing Line Press
PO Box 1626
Georgetown, Kentucky 40324
USA

Table of Contents

I. Crucible
- Grandmother's Photo ... 1
- The Red Dress ... 2
- Hey Lou ... 3
- Eden Vanished ... 4

II. Lessons Learned
- First Teacher ... 5
- Bible School ... 6
- Look ... 7
- Creak Walks ... 8
- Rocky Mountain Campfire Girls ... 9
- The Linguist ... 10
- Three Doll Houses ... 11
- Ode to the Blank Page ... 12

III. Strategies
- Getting By ... 13
- Happiness ... 14
- Riding the Sphinx ... 15
- The Meerkat and the Otter ... 16
- Farm for Bitter Women ... 17
- School Daze ... 18

IV. Shadows
- The Phoenix ... 19
- Confession ... 20
- First Death ... 21
- Silence ... 22
- Sunday Afternoon Drama ... 23
- Entertainment ... 24
- The Turning ... 25

V. Coming to Terms
- Jewels for Marian ... 27
- Our Garden ... 28
- My Pittsburgh ... 29
- Home is not lost ... 30
- Circling Back ... 31

I. CRUCIBLE

Grandma's Photo

My father is the baby in her arms up to his neck in a white christening gown,
  richly embroidered and flowing down over her floor length dark skirt.
Her blouse, stark white against the photo's brown tints, collars her neck just
  below her chin.
Arms, hidden in puffy sleeves, cradle the baby.
A dark cloud of hair rests on her forehead and a French braid runs up the
  back of her head.
Her face is smooth with a young girl's dreams as she smiles adoringly
  at my father.
This is before.
Before her lusty husband disappeared for days at a time with his coronet and
  his umpah band.
Before she heard the whispers and the fights began
Before he lost his leg in a gas field explosion and dragged them down into
  poverty
Before she took her beloved son out of school at fifteen and send him off to
  work
Before she opened her house to boarders
Before her lips grew hard and pursed in worry and shame
Before she learned how hard it is just to keep going.

The Red Dress

The dress was as bright red as her lipstick, the neckline embroidered
    in gold threads
 the skirt swept the floor, the earrings glowed.
Her gold shoes were spiked
    with slender heels.
Mother never wore high heels. She wore blue jeans and tennis shoes.
True, Sundays she wore a navy-blue suit and
    a black dress for Christmas and Thanksgiving.
But now she had rouge on her cheeks and smelled of perfume.
Tonight, my mother was beautiful.
Smiling down at her, Dad took her arm, and swept her out the door.
She never dressed up again.
She never bought herself any new clothes that I could tell.
I guess she didn't want to be beautiful anymore.
She cooked, listened to our chatter,
and kept a garden with as many flowers as vegetables.
She raised my brother and me, helped raise her brother's two boys
    and her son's two children.
She was useful.
She could have had a career in genetics.
She could have been beautiful
She chose otherwise.

Hey, Great Grandma Lou

Louisiana Richey, nee Ditch—born to a German, married to a Scot, a combination to toughen up any woman, I could have picked your daughter Alma, the would-be opera star, feminist, and mother to four but you are more fun. Alma is painted with sorrow. It seeped into her bones.

Your picture is on my laptop and I smile at you every night. Little round lady, smiling back surrounded by Tot and Alma, her husband Jim, Harry who is Jim's brother, Harry's wife who is Alma's sister and maybe John or Blair. I want to crawl into the picture and beg a hug.

Did you fall for John Richey's uniform when he returned from the Civil War at your father's side? Did he have a uniform? Did your father, Jerimiah, approve? Did your stepmother help you pack your bags when you left Indiana for Kansas? Did your sister Missouri cry when you left? Where was Alma conceived? Where did you met Fanny who would cook and manage Alma and then her four?

Mom said you laughed a lot. I guess that got you through. What grit you had, following your husband from Indiana, to Kansas, to New Mexico to Texas, homesteading then selling up to go to the next great opportunity. Sort of like flipping houses. You raised five children on the journey and your husband did well in real estate, but Tot never married, Blair committed suicide and the other boys' children were wiped out by World War II.

Still, thanks to Alma and Jim, you have great, great, great grandchildren, five in Japan and two in South Dakota, a couple on the east coast, one in Illinois, three in Florida, three in Texas and two here in Pennsylvania.

Alma did something right.

I would love to hear your stories. Mom said you were a great storyteller.

I miss you.

Lost Eden

I swam in the warmth of your love
Took crystal bits of raw turnip you'd carved out with your pocket knife,
 a mouthful of peas scooped out of their pod with your big thumb,
 a bite of sun-warmed tomato
 juice running down my chin,
as we walked through Mom's garden.

Try this, know this, look here, listen.
You anointed me with books, newspapers, magazines, encyclopedias,
Blessed me with music,
Seeped me in your pride.

In time, you pushed me off your lap
 And I turned out of the light.

II. LESSONS LEARNED

First Teacher

Mother was an entomologist
She knew important things
She could dissect an earthworm on the sidewalk
And describe its parts for our rapacious friends
When she killed a chicken for dinner
She gave a formal lecture on its heart and lungs and digestive system
It was hard to argue with her about germy candy on the floor
Licking it off certainly wasn't the answer.
Leftovers from dinner were whipped into the refrigerator
And never kept for over three days
Beware the potato salad left on the picnic table for hours
Germs were everywhere and they could kill you
She would explain and show pictures
Cuts were serious and staining iodine or mercurochrome were used lavishly
Even eighty years later I eye the well-refrigerated mayo with suspicion
And marvel that my grandchildren still live
Considering how their mothers seem unaware of germs.

Bible School

God weighted good and evil, one in one hand, one in the other
They were equal.
That hadn't worked out so well on the last planet so
She tipped a little of the evil out
Smeared them over the Earth and said,
"Let's see how that works out."
Then she started the process, rolling out the seas, blowing the winds,
Forming the mountains as she gave one good push to the
Tectonic Plates.
She brushed her hands back and forth three times
Then left.

Look

God herself is invisible, only miracles are discernable
Miracles are:
    A baby picking up a bead between thumb and index finger
    The swift rush of green in spring
    A sky paved with stars, every star a promise
    The way waves keep coming and coming and coming
    The way lightening fills the entire bowl of the sky in Kansas
    The way a smile lights a gloomy face
    The way a child's laugh echoes in my chest.
It is a miracle someone figured how to build a cathedral, or a skyscraper or a house.
It is a miracle a whole city of traffic moves this way and that way without too much fuss.
It is miracle a hundred musicians work a lifetime to come together and play a symphony.
It is a miracle Wilber and Orville got off their bicycles and tossed us into the sky.

Creak Walks

Freed from the cabin with an hour till the next activity
We scattered down the grassy sleeve of slope, sun hot on our backs.
Jane and I, the youngest campers, headed for the wooden bridge
Hinged to the creek on either side.
We scrambled over planks hot on our bare feet
To the other side for easy access to the water,
We slid down the mud-paved hollow to the cool.
From tall trees on either side heavy leaved branches
Met over the creek making us a bower,
Our home here in this alien country called Camp.
Carefully choosing the flattest rocks
We stepped into the burbling stream
A fairyland of dark water with bits of sparkle
Walled by anonymous bushes. vines, poison ivy and jewelweed
With translucent stems and seed pods that begged for popping
Shifting from stone to stone
Then slipping into the mud-bottomed water slime slipping between our toes
We climbed to the place where blackberry's bushes
Bent over the stream handing us ripe black fruit.
A little ways up was a grassy bank
Where we sat to savor our prize as juice glazed our chins.
Next, we knelt by the stream washing hands and faces
The cool water singing to our skin
Then upending rocks to make rooms,
With sticks, pebbles, leaves, and flowers, we built our fairy houses
And played out fairy stories till the camp bell rang
Calling us back to their reality.

Rocky Mountain Campfire Girls

Up in the foothills beyond Denver
Shaded by trees lay our brown wooden cabins for sleeping,
    A hall for dining room or theater
      Stables for horses and washrooms with showers
Above the hall was the Bluebird cabin.
Finished with second grade they came with their teddy bears
    Found their bunks along with two wranglers in tight jeans and tall hats
      Two counselors and me, Boss of the Bluebirds, Director of singing.
Below, in front of the hall
A wide spread of grass, a flag pole, a huge bell, and fire pit
    Shivering, before the sun found us, we circled the flag pole
    As the trumpeter played Reveille, we sang the flag up
Through dark forest, thin paths took us to stables, craft house and
 Up to the hilltop displaying green valleys and sharp mountain peaks
        Evenings were spent in the hall hearing stories, singing, and dancing
        Ended with Taps.
We campers slept one night a week in bedrolls under a vast dome of stars
Bluebirds walked down to camp in front of the hall
    Like big girls they rolled their own bedrolls
    With blankets, a sheet, and canvas for ground cover.
Their knots were loose, always gave way
Spilling sheets and blankets and contraband
     Like pillows or teddy bears
     Or sometimes some candy
Hard to leave at the end of the summer, harder to refuse to return
To aspen and columbine, stars and sheer cliffs, smell of hot pine resin
     But I knew there was more beauty to find: Banff, Montreal, Cape Breton,
      Wales, Glasgow. St. John's, New Orleans, the Outer Banks, Arcadia. . .

The Linguist

From hot green sun into cool black tunnel come four adventurers,
Tiny mother chasing seven-year-old Joey, racing, testing the echo,
Wide father riding three-year-old Lysbeth on his shoulders.

Long tunnel walls are lit by picture windows filled with a rainbow of fish,
        next the sleek dark ominous sharks.
Joey hunts for a way round the glass. "I could swim with them."
Father chants biology lessons.
Lysbeth looks and looks.

Rounding the last gloomy corner, they find a fantasy in black and white.
While Joey slips under the rail to touch the glass, the rest slip into wonder.

Penguins waddle on ice. Penguins slide into water and dance.

Lysbeth breaks the silence, "Bird."
        Bends her head to one side, "Fish."
                Straightens up and nods in decision, "Man."
Wonder shifts to her busy mind.
Father and Mother are silent before this mystery.

Three Doll Houses

Childless, I made three doll houses and a fairy house of all of clay.
Onto the doll house roof, I pasted slivers of balsa wood for shingles
Sewed little curtains, bed covers, sheets, even tiny pillow covers
Cut out intricate rugs from magazines
Glued together little chairs and tables, stained dark brown
Drenched in the joy of making.
You all looked at me in puzzlement that said,
        "What can I do with this?"
You enjoyed our dyeing thousands of Easter eggs, and decorating dozens of
gingerbread houses
      with sticky candies, and pasty frosting in vivid blues,
greens, and reds,
        making messes on your mothers' tables.
I carefully chose piles of books and gifts for you at each birthday and
Christmas.
Now
I think you mostly needed me to be me.

Ode to the Blank Page

Here's to the blank page
The new day
The new year
The first day at school, at work, at marriage, at birth
Here's to all the new beginnings.
The make-up after the fight
The end of a long flight
Stepping off the plane into another place
Here's to starting over after failure
Picking up the old pieces, finding new
Here's to a new face swimming into view
Friend or foe to be
Here's to a new reality after loss
Loss of a limb, a parent, a spouse, a child
How to go on
What to put on that blank page
Thanks be to the blessing of a new page.

III. STRATEGIES

Getting By

What does the humming bird feel
As it dips its forked tongue deep into the flower's sticky heart?
Sweet and rushing energy?
Or can it finally relax for a millisecond, as though at home
Here in just this bowl of tissue it is made for
Then, in a short bit of time, off to find another
Wandering here, there
Searching, always searching
Always ready to fight the bumble bee for liquid gold.

The great cats do not flit
They wait behind tall grasses
Or a jungle's vines and tree trunks
Or around some craggy mountain corner
They crawl slowly toward the goal of continued life
Then pounce.

Happiness

Three-year-old Cynthia dancing, arms out, hair flying, laughing.
Barbara pulling the cauliflower pie from the oven.
It's cheesy top a perfect golden brown.
Fred sitting in his garden of flowers and vegetables watching his goldfish
As he listens to the sprinkle of water flowing over his fountain of rocks
In his iris framed pond.
Sarah finding a student loves the class she is teaching.
Marian loving and laughing at the foibles of her neighbors
Lysbeth learning her book of poems will be published
Robert sunk in the beauty of the aria.
Jean eating chocolates.
Happiness comes in all colors.

Riding the Sphinx

Sarah and Grandmother make gray pyramids of clay.

They bake dull jewels of Fimo for the tomb, Indiana's treasure.
They write a story at the computer sitting together in the black office chair.
In the story they ride the friendly Sphinx
The Great Pyramid points the way.

Sarah at seven grapples with death and builds an obsession of Egypt.
Is she planning to wrap herself in bandages and live forever? Grandmother wonders.
I'm going to be an archeologist and find treasure. Sarah knows.

What pearls is Sarah layering from the grit in her rich life?

The Meerkat and the Otter

Meerkat and Otter follow me everywhere.

Otter slithers along the floor looking endlessly for ways to play.

Meerkat is on guard wherever. Whisking here and there hunting for danger.

We go down to Kathy's salon to have my hair chopped.

Otter slides into the rinsing tub and splashes Kathy as she washes my hair.

Meerkat stands at the door watching then runs to check out the backroom with the poisonous chemicals that change your hair to straight or curly, black or red or blond. Then into the bathroom.

Otter follows him into the bathroom, dips in the toilet, then slides around in the sink, then out.

Dion comes in for her afternoon chores. Mrs. Williams is coming to have her nails glorified. Otter and Meerkat rush to check out this tubby blond creation. They follow behind her for a minute or two then turn away for more interesting activities.

Otter curls into the cat's cushy basket for a nap

Meerkat stands at the door watching.

Farm for Bitter Women

Let us grow cucumbers on vines
Watch tiny thumbs with wee prickles grow
We should stake out red tomatoes and green peppers,
Hide little potato eyes in the ground
Then hunt for new potatoes down deep in dirt
Let us have nasturtiums all fluttery orange or yellow
Red zinnias stiff with importance
Teasing cosmos, delicate in pink
We must have bright bee balm, cone flower, black-eyed susan, foxglove.
We will beg the Queen Anne's lace to stay
With all the daisies, jewelweed, spikes of goldenrod.
Bees, butterflies and hummingbirds will swirl around us
We will lie down in soft grass and watch clouds paint us pictures
Our bitterness will leach into the earth.

School Daze

Here is where I waited on the corner for the bus in the 70's
    Across on that corner you could buy drugs
    Behind me an old lady sat at her window making sure I was safe.

On the other side of the street is a large school building
    Constructed when the wealthy lived two streets over
    Large windows, ornate stairways, the best of the times.

Not far behind the school building were boarded up row houses
    Where lost children hid at night in the attics
    Where lost adults hunted for solace down below.

Inside the school was the office where the principal hid
    Behind his door and a fierce secretary
    Wearing a gamblers cap so no one could see his eyes.

Just down from him was a happy classroom papered with crayoned dreams
    Managed by a miracle in a flowered house dress
    Where children laughed and learned.

Two blocks up were old mansions of departed wealthy
    Being scraped and pounded by a courageous few
    To bring them back to life.

And just within sight was a new building housing promise
    A man determined to save a few
    Offered hope and art.

IV. SHADOWS

The Phoenix

The Universe shifted
Heaven opened up and Dad bent down to talk to me
Death winked.
A courtly herald appeared to shout the news,
A trumpeter dressed in green and black, with a red feather in his cap.
The crowd trembled and turned away.
Drenched in an erasing rain, turning to celluloid, I stumbled on.
The rooms were empty.
Day after day, month moved on to another month.
Sparkling fairy dust sprinkled the people and they forgot.
But the shift was permanent.
I was somebody else. Nobody knew. Not even me

Confession

Sorry, I confess. I don't remember where I was when I heard about JFK
I remember sitting in a dim room once with pale light shining on our radio.
The warm wood of its sides peeked in a gentle arch.
We were all watching the radio as FDR spoke about infamy.
Mom said, "Well, that does it."
Dad said, "Nothing else to do."
I stopped listening. They always argued about the news. I was seven.
I remember a Saturday at Friend's camp.
We had spent a week learning about the world, grown-up stuff. I was seventeen.
We were on a path in the woods talking and laughing
Someone ran up to us waving a paper.
The headline read, *Korea Invaded.*
My heart stopped. I knew we would soon die in a nuclear war.
I don't remember much about the Bay of Pigs, or how we got caught up in Vietnam.
It's just been horror on top of horror.

First Death

"Help me," a low rumble from the lump that is my father,
    smothered in sheets of a hospital bed.
Holding a hand, I lean to kiss his cheek
    and hear only beeps dancing in the air.
The family dragons snatch me away and cast me from his dying.
"Clean the house for company" is my command,
Going from best beloved to Cinders in the ashes.
The week trudges on forever, the dragons towing me behind them
The Undertaker speaks in capitols
The town wanders through his lair
They speak in platitudes, the room is full of mutterings, a laugh, an occasional half-sob
An old lady kneels on the floor, beside the coffin.
The Undertaker is forced across the street to borrow a kneeler from the Catholic Undertaker.
Mother pulls on her role every morning and falls into silence at night
After three days in his pine box, he is rolled into the fire.
Mother takes him home in a tin box. Neither speak.
I wander into the rest of my life.

Silence

Why won't you answer your phone?
I need to hear your voice, my otherside.
It's been ten years now your phone went dead
I wanted to talk to you yesterday when the storm ran up Florida's coast.
Share our joy, on Sanibel.
Waiting out the sunrise, on the beach just beyond the silver, sea-soaked wood.
Hunting for shells at the four AM low tide
The Vodka Story
You crawling to the dinner table on your hands and knees
Me sharing too much even though Eleanora was listening
Where did you go?
I need you to bounce against, to know who I am.

Sunday Afternoon Drama

Aunt Mae brought the baked beans and Uncle Timothy had lighted the charcoal for the franks and hamburg and now stood over the grill a spatula in one hand a beer in the other watching the sizzling meat.

The buns sat wrapped in plastic waiting with the mustard, Heinz Catsup, and mayo, chopped onions, chopped hot peppers, sliced tomatoes. There was potato salad beside the deviled eggs, all covered of course. Plastic knives, forks and spoons lay beside paper plates. napkins and cups.

Cousins Peter and Daryl wrestled on the ground giggling till Daryl twisted Peter's arm a little too far and he went weeping to his mother the sissy.

Little Marie was allowed to carry out the iced tea jug.

A barrel of ice was filled with pop and beer in one corner of the yard.

Aunt Lucy and Aunt Rita were gossiping again in another.

Eddie was bringing out the old boom box for some music.

The baby started crying and Tilly picked him up to take him inside where it was cooler. Momma Jolene waited at the top of the porch stairs till she passed and then came down the stairs carrying a white platter with a high mound of fried chicken.

No one noticed the gunmen behind the fence till the shooting started.

Red splattered everywhere, even on the plastic covering the deviled eggs.

Entertainment

They brought the hospital bed into our living room.
My husband would never leave it. He couldn't stand or even sit in a wheelchair.
I slept beside him on the couch, managed with aides and Hospice, took his sugar readings, feed him as much as he would eat. He loved the cups of chocolate ice cream. Washed and dressed him and changed his diaper.
He didn't like to listen to music anymore, but watched sports or America's Favorite Home Videos on TV, sometimes old movies. He liked Second World War movies, the Navy ones.
I always kept the TV on.
Mostly, he slept.
It was morning, September eleventh. I thought it was some movie when I passed by the TV
Then I saw it was real.
"Look, Fred,"
I sat and watched the horror all day.
I'm not sure that Fred didn't think it was a movie.
Like when I told him his son Mark was dead. I'm not sure what went in.
But then for me, Fred's slow dying was real
and the planes smashing into buildings could have been a movie.

The Turning

Jumping from celebration to celebration
We spend our year in anticipation of future joy
From New Year's Eve to Valentine's Day
From champagne and fireworks to hearts and chocolates
    From St. Patrick's Day to Easter
    From green parades to colored eggs
        From May Day to Weddings and Graduations
        From flowers to ceremonies and gifts
            From Fourth of July to Vacation Days
            From fireworks and picnics to searching for escape
                From Thanksgiving to Christmas
                From groaning tables to evergreens and mistletoe
And back to New Year's Day/
Do we ever think to remember
Carrying the moon with us, we circle the sun and turn through regulated changes?
        I hang six calendars on my walls, so I won't forget but
            remember to hunt for the full moon from my window
            remember to step out into the spring rain to smell the opulent loam

We fight the heat in the summer and the cold in the winter
With armor of clothes, machines blowing fake cool, tumbling ice at a touch.
Our bodies learn to ignore the feel of the natural rise and fall, cold to hot,

What to us is the earth's warming, the seas rising, the glaciers melting?
        We have constructed a reality out of pulp and fractured oil,
the well-aged bones of our ancestors
                and turn our backs to the milky way.

V. COMING TO TERMS

Jewels for Marian

When we were seventeen you grumbled
"Why do only old ladies get real jewels to wear?
Jewels look better against young skin."
Now at eighty we sit in our sapphires and diamonds
watching young girls go by unadorned
slim bodies molded into magnets for the eye.
Today, I declare the distribution of jewels altogether fitting.

Our Garden

The garden we made here all those years together
It echoes with laughter
Contains growing things of all ages
Tiny ones just pushing up out of the ground, sending pale slender roots
    Digging down, finding purchase
Some full grown producing myriad fruits and lush nuts.
One withered and died for no good reason.
Those seeds you blew out of your restless mind
    into the rolling breeze landed in
        nameless places and flourished or didn't.
We have not heard
Our garden is still green. I water it as I can and the sun shines every day
We sit surrounded by living riches although you drifted away some time ago
Do you watch us grow, expand, droop, revive and go on?
We catch a glimpse of you just beyond the trellis.
    Come over and hold my hand.

My Pittsburgh

Pittsburgh isn't an old city like Athens, Greece
   or a young city like Wichita, Kansas,
Maybe an old-young city, finding its feet, evaluating its possibilities,
   deciding to go on or fade away.
Growing up, a month-long visitor in my aunt's house every year
Pittsburgh was my summer playground
   running down hillside steps
   playing in the dirty blackening hillside woods
   smelling the soft bitter smell of crushed ailanthus leaves,
   alien tree of heaven
   teeth rattling roller skating on Belgium blocks that
   smoothed out onto warm asphalt
   swinging round in the revolving doors of the Carnegie Museum
   sharing the cool with the long black bones of our dinosaurs
   sitting on the terrace at dusk, waiting for the houses below to light up.
The mills were alive then, throwing out fire.
Did everyone walk faster? I ran.
I went to a Pittsburgh college,
      found a husband here, a family, cheered for Panthers, Pirates,
Steelers, Penguins
      learned to find: West End, Northside, Oakland, Squirrel Hill,
Blawnox, Sheraden,
      Fairywood, Regent Square, Shadyside, Lemington, Carrick.
Now here I am melting into old age, running no more.
  never to miss the crisp bright football falls and weepy sneezy, flowery
springs
   nor dirty sturdy brick homes surrounded by green, green, green
   nor a Gothic cathedral, a gothic skyscraper, and a Greek Temple
      all plopped down together
   nor the nighttime sky blazing against the dark hills.
No. I will dare the ice of winter and the steam of summer to say,
      "Pittsburgh is my home."
I am a rooted alien, crushed soft and bitter, evaluating my possibilities,
   deciding whether to go on or fade away.

Home Is Not Lost

Home is where you know where you are
Not lost
        Lost is wandering a street not sure where you are
        or how to find your way to some place
        Lost is holding your husband's hand as he is dying.
        The connection breaks.
        You are floating free.
        Lost is standing in the pulpit at a funeral
        wondering how you got there
        Seeing all those faces looking up
        Wondering what you were going to say
Home is where your feet fall on solid ground
        Where you know every nook
        Where you know where everything is or where it might be
        Or knowing it is there somewhere.
Home has walls that shelter and pin
        With a door that can open on promise or threat
Menacing unknown or
        Fresh wind blowing and warm sun
        Somewhere an ocean rolls in and out
        Somewhere daffodils bloom and tulips are pushing up
        Somewhere else.

Circling Back

Where are those happy little Disney birds when you need them?
They could do the dishes every night like he did.
They could make my bed and scrub my floors, tweeting all the while.
And throw out all the stuff I don't want.
They're magic. They know what I don't want.

Where is the handsome prince, well maybe a retired old king?
Old King Cole was a merry ol' soul. He might do.
We could go to movies or out to dinner or find those three fiddlers and
watch the dancing.

How about you find me a goose,
One of those golden egg layers, but I don't want to mess with giants.
Maybe I could have just one golden fleece or a tub of spun gold
Or one rub of the lantern.

I want to lie on Bagheera's smooth black back and tell him about my day.
I want to sleep in the soft fur of Baloo's arms.

Jean Fleischauer worked for thirty-some years teaching in an elementary school and then working as a school psychologist in the Pittsburgh Public Schools. When she retired, she began to study fiction writing and poetry. Jean was blessed with many good teachers in formal classes and informal writing groups. She has only recently begun to attempt publication.

www.ingramcontent.com/pod-product-compliance
Lightning Source LLC
Chambersburg PA
CBHW022125090426
42743CB00008B/1016